# THE GOLDEN INVITATION

Written and Illustrated by

**Ryoon Wha Kang**

e-book ISBN: 978-1-3999-0621-0
Paperback ISBN: 978-1-3999-0620-3



Publication designed by Josiah Yechan Kim

I dedicate this book to my children yet to be born,
my loving husband who supported me with invaluable
encouragement and advice in producing this book,
and my parents who are always on my side.

One day, the grandpa dragonfly
was resting on a tree branch.

He saw a little girl and asked,
"Why are you downcast?"

The little girl replied,
"I didn't get to say goodbye to my friend."

The grandpa dragonfly asked,
"Who is your special friend?"

The little girl replied,
“Well, he is as soft as the cloud, as fast as the wind, but as adventurous as a sailor! No rain and no snow can stop him!”

The grandpa dragonfly suggested,
“Why don’t you borrow these wings
to find him? Quick, you better hurry!”

The little girl beamed with excitement and said,
"Wow! Thank you grandpa dragonfly."

The grandpa dragonfly continued,
"Just remember to pass these wings to another downcast soul afterwards."

"Okay I will grandpa dragonfly!"
The little girl answered.

Up and up the little girl

soared into the sky.

Through the clouds the little girl found
her special friend and she whispered,

“Good bye, balloon.”

The little girl did not need the wings anymore. She looked around and found a caterpillar.

"Why are you downcast?"
The little girl asked.

The caterpillar answered,
"If only I can fly from one flower to another, drinking plenty of nectar!
I think life is too short to be trapped in a chrysalis."

The little girl suggested,
“Why don’t you take these wings to fly from one flower to another to find nectar? Then you don’t have to wait to become a butterfly!”

The caterpillar replied,
"What a brilliant idea! Thank you."

The little girl said,
"Just remember to pass these wings to another downcast soul afterwards."

The caterpillar replied,
"Okay, will do!"

The caterpillar flew to different flowers,
having the most colourful feasts everyday.

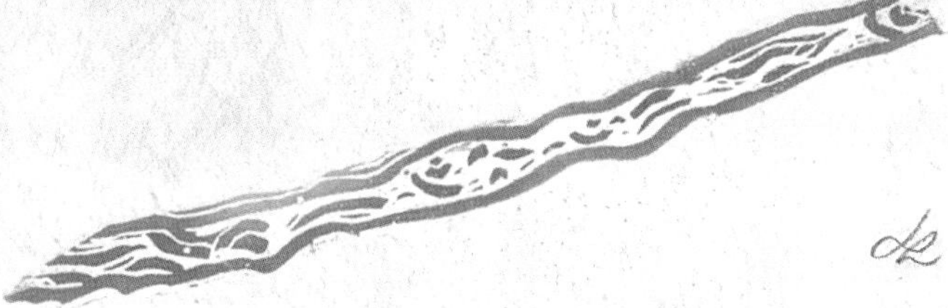

While the caterpillar was munching,
a butterfly came and said,
"It is you! It really is you! We were
caterpillars together, remember?
Why are you still a caterpillar?"

The caterpillar replied,
"Well, I have been living my life to the full.
I have everything I need, as I can fly and
munch my way into any nectar I want."

The butterfly said,
"I see, but life as a butterfly is not about what you have or don't have. It is about the pollen that you carry for the flowers. Also, nectar is given as a present, not taken whenever you want to. Anyway, I've got work to do. See you!"

The caterpillar watched the butterfly gracefully fly away. Then the thought of having work to share pollen for flowers excited him.

The caterpillar didn't need the wings
anymore, so he looked around.

He saw a turtle and asked,
"Mr. Turtle, why are you downcast?"

Mr. Turtle answered,
"I want to go beyond the mangrove forest, but I am too afraid."

The caterpillar laughed and said,
"Nonsense! You have the best armour. What are you afraid of? You can also walk on land and swim in water!"

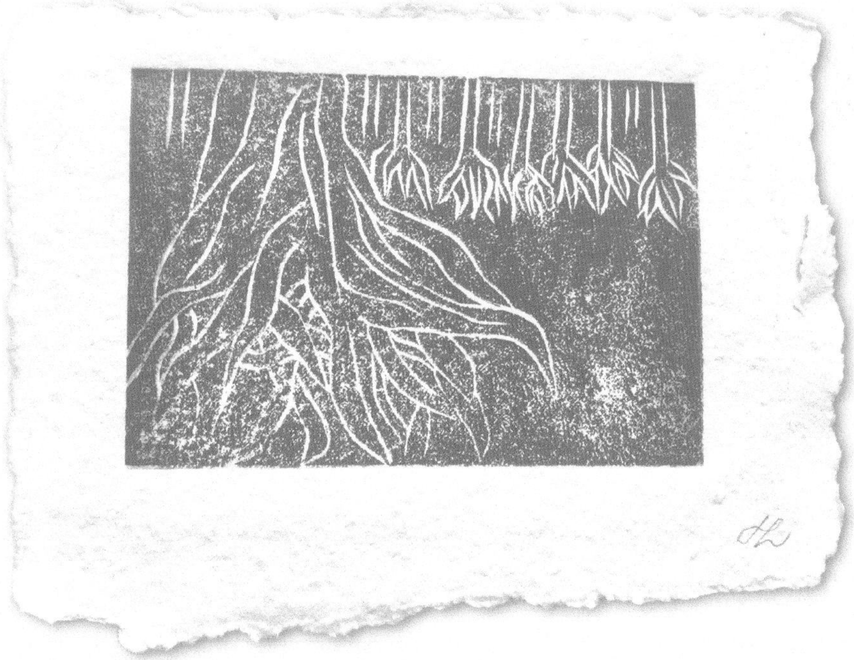

Mr. Turtle said,
“I am too slow to run away when I
am scared. I am used to hiding in my
shell, but I am always so curious.”

"Why don't you take these wings to
make you faster then?"
The caterpillar challenged Mr. Turtle.

After a moment of silence,
Mr. Turtle replied,

"I need time to think."

"Well, I have no time to spare."
The caterpillar said,
"I will leave these wings here for you
to take whenever you are ready. Bye!"

The caterpillar hung the wings on the
branch and turned into a chrysalis.

Mr. Turtle pondered for a while.
When the chrysalis started to show
the changing caterpillar, or the new
butterfly, Mr. Turtle took the wings.

Mr. Turtle's heart pounded as he was flying across the mangrove forest.

'What could there be?' Mr. Turtle thought. 'Will there be monsters? In which case, should I flap the wings harder to turn back or hide in my shell until they disappear?'

As soon as he turned the corner, his eyes were shut tightly by the bright rays of the sun, shining directly at him from the open sky.

The gentle breeze brushed his neck
and carried off his sweat.
In return, it brought back
the whiff of fragrance
that led him to water lilies,
clothed in colours
as charming as its scent.

The breeze skilfully shook the mangrove trees in the distance, playing rustling music with the leaves.

Mr. Turtle relaxed.

He enjoyed meeting other creatures, none of which looked like monsters. His heart was content and curiosity was fulled. He didn't need the wings anymore. In fact, he wanted to take a slow stride back home.

Mr. Turtle however, realised that the caterpillar didn't tell him where and how to return the wings!

'The caterpillar would have turned into a butterfly and flown away by now.' Thought Mr. Turtle. 'Surely though,' continued Mr. Turtle, the wings should be passed onto a downcast soul.'

"So then," Mr. Turtle asks,
"Where will you go with these wings?"

## About the Author

R Kang is a full time doctor working for the National Health Service in the U.K. On a daily basis she comes across many priceless moments, memories and inspirations, which prompted her to start capturing them and birthed a desire to voice these with the wider world expressed through her writing and relief printing. Stories are inspired by those shared by people around her that she then reminds them back during times of difficulty, agony, confusion and sometimes, frankly speaking, flickering memory. She not only loves living life but also life that comes in all shapes and sizes in the plant and animal kingdom, which is reflected in her stories.

Printed in Great Britain
by Amazon

72488429R00033